Sharon's Collection Of Poems

By Sharon Wiegand

Sharon's Book

www.Sharonsbook.com

In the Country

It is beautiful in the mountains of Colorado

The summer time has winding springs

Through the middle of the canyons

Near the houses by the banks of the springs.

There are working cattle near the green hills

And there is such easy living near by

Where they have barbeques

And compete in bull riding and rope handling.

The authenticity of the beauty of towns

Spread around the grassy northeast

Comes to life when the cowboys

Find their way to the soda shops downtown.

By: Sharon Wiegand

God Created Us

What hath God created?

But a place where we can reside

He's set forth our lives

The way they should be

And all we need to do

Is following his words.

He's brought us along

His path of righteousness

And given us his redemption

As long as we believe in him

We have our lives

Set up for us.

Believe in me,

And my son Jesus

He told the world

Spread my message

As you go

And miracles will happen.

By: Sharon Wiegand

Bearded Men

Have you ever tried to kiss a bearded man?

It's so scratchy and it makes red marks

All over your face.

The men think it looks sexy on them

But they never know how it feels to a woman.

I think they look like homeless men

And I would rather not be around them,

But for some reason

They think it make them look more manly.

I hope my man

Never wears a beard

Because it is so scratchy

And it breaks out my face.

By: Sharon Wiegand

Jesus Words

John 14: 27-29

I am leaving you with a gift

Peace of mind and heart.

And the peace I give is a gift the world cannot give

So don't be troubled or afraid.

Remember what I told you

I am going away

I will come back to you again.

If you really love me,

You would be happy that I am going to the Father,

Who is greater than I am?

I have told you these things

Before they happen

So that when they do happen,

You will believe

NASCAR

NASCAR is my favorite sport

We watch the drivers as they speed on by

We root for our favorite driver as he zooms

Down the speedway.

Will he get in a crash or will he get bumped

From the back?

As he rams his car down the road

His opponents give him dirty looks.

Because he's won so many races

And they know he might win this one.

Here he comes around the bend

And sure enough he wins by a second.

By: Sharon Wiegand

Many Nights

Many nights I lie there awake

I think about my Savior

And if he's watching me.

I know he's up their somewhere

And I know he's thinking about me

But I hope he knows I'm sincere.

I sometimes have a complex problem

I don't think a lot of myself

I know it's because of the way I was raised.

I need to get over it

That's why I come to God

I know he will heal me

From all my weary woes.

By: Sharon Wiegand

Jitterbug

My sister taught me the jitterbug

When I was very young

As she watched the

Dick Clark Show on TV.

There were many guests

On the show

But the same dancers

Were always there to perform.

I kept up with her

As she glided around the floor

It was a pleasure

To dance with my sister as a partner.

By: Sharon Wiegand

Medicare

They want to cut our Medicare

I hope they will be there

When their mothers and fathers

Are suffering and dying.

Maybe the rich congressmen

Can afford to sustain

Their families

But what do the poor do.

I would hate to watch people die

And know that I was a part of it

When I could help the seniors

Get their benefits they deserve.

By: Sharon Wiegand

Killing

Our soldiers are killing people every day

And other people are killing us.

Why?

There must be a better way.

Our soldier come back maimed

Their minds are destroyed from killing

What are we doing to these young men?

They don't deserve this.

I don't know what the answer is

But there must be a better way

Killing can't be the answer

We must resolve this more simply.

By: Sharon Wiegand

Stuttering

I knew a man who always stuttered

But he met this wonderful

Girl and he never stuttered

When he was around her.

Any other time he always stuttered

But the minute she entered

The room

He never stuttered a word.

By: Sharon Wiegand

Depression Does Hold You Back

Depression does hold you back

I've found that out in many ways

It makes you into a different person

And you can't control your behavior.

It makes you feel like suicide

It gives you extreme migraines

Sometimes it gives you mania, bipolar,

And seizures.

It causes nausea, dizziness, sweating

It makes you feel sad, helpless.

But most of the time

You feel ok as long as you take medicine.

By: Sharon Wiegand

The Calm before the Tornado

Every Time in Oklahoma we had a tornado

It would get very quiet

It was so quiet that you could almost hear a pin drop

Before the tornado would hit.

The sky would get very dark

Almost black in color

And you knew something was going to happen

Then the city buzzer would ring

And you knew you only

Had a few minutes to get

To a cellar or to a basement

Or get somewhere to safety before it hit.

And then you would close your eyes

And hope and pray everyone would be safe,

Not only their property but their lives.

By: Sharon Wiegand

Trust in the Lord

I trust in the Lord each day

He keeps me going as I pray

I love to look out the window

And see what has come to day.

He is my special guide along the way.

I love to hear his voice

I know he is up there somewhere

He grants me so much every day.

He is my rock, my soul, my Lord, and my Savior.

By: Sharon Wiegand

Jesus is calling

Jesus is calling

He is calling me home

I hear his voice each and every day

He says I'm coming home.

Near the end you will know

He calls your name

You know you will be by his side

And wearing a white robe.

In revelations it says

You will be wearing a white robe

And you will be beside him

Only the ones who believe in him

Will be there.

By: Sharon Wiegand

Confidence

My friend has so much confidence

She is so dignified and respectable

I wish I could be as remarkable as she is

But it will never happen.

She is such a gracious lady

We were best friends when we were children

When I was having problems with my parents

She came and saw me and brought me a birthday cake.

Even though I have not seen her in years

I know she has that same quality that she always had

She cheers me up all the time

And inspires me just at the right times.

By: Sharon Wiegand

Happiness I Share

The happiness I share I find at church

The members always have a smile

The chorus sings beautiful music

And our service dog greets us at the door.

I love to sing out of the old song books

And listen to different people read passages out of the bible

And to give the offering

And listen to the Pastor.

Sunday is my favorite day of the week

I get to be with the Lord

My husband

And the people at church.

By: Sharon Wiegand

Starry Skies

Among the starry skies

Are beautiful stars mixed with clouds of white?

They show the background of blue

That guides us close to God.

God is you there?

We have the faith and the answers

You gave us that you do exist

And we believe you are there.

Come to us

And take our hands and guide us

To the promise land

And we will be clothed in white robes.

By: Sharon Wiegand

God, You Are My Savior

I pray every day

That you will come for me

You are my spirit

And my soul.

I love my Lord

I believe in what he says

I will be waiting

For when he comes for me.

By: Sharon Wiegand

Guide Dogs

The guide Dogs are special
They take care of special people
They know that many need them
And their love helps them too.

They do what people can't do
They see what some people can't
They help people cross the street
And save them from harm.

These dogs will never forsake you
They are kind in every way
They do all the things other dogs won't do
I love to watch them work.

By: Sharon Wiegand

Rejuvenate Your Skin

The youthfulness of your skin

Stays looking nice

When you continue to

Take care of your skin.

With age, it loses its appeal

So you must kept it clean

Soft, and washed

Breathtaking from within.

Use a few active ingredients

That will keep your skin soft

But make sure your face is clean

And you will always be beautiful.

By: Sharon Wiegand

Numerous Children

Many celebrities are adopting

From faraway places

What about from our country.

I wish I was adopted when I was a child

Instead of going through all the abuse

I went through.

I bet a lot of children would rather

Be adopted by someone like you

Than go through what they are

Going through.

By: Sharon Wiegand

New Zealand

The climate in New Zealand is

Chilly at night, warm in the day

They are very friendly people

Who eat a lot of mutton?

The grass is waist high through hilly country

They drink warm beer while

Eating tough stringy beef and

They are very proud of their country.

By: Sharon Wiegand

Germany

Still run on the Audubon.

Beautiful mountains in the area

The main meal is at noon, with a

Light breakfast, and light dinner.

Great train system connects in the whole country.

They are very friendly people.

They have a lot of castles to visit.

They drink warm beer which is considered bread.

The only good beer is made in churches.

The only drunk people are visitors.

They have a lot of museums.

No crime, no welfare.

By: Sharon Wiegand

Stay True to Yourself

Always do what you think is best

I used to always follow what everyone else did

And that was a big mistake.

You must do what you feel is right

No matter what anyone else thinks

Following someone else just gets you in trouble.

I found that out so many times.

Just stay true to yourself and everything will be ok.

By: Sharon Wiegand

Our Charming Utah

There are so many natural wonders

Contained in the five national

Parks which include Zion, Bryce Canyon,

Capitol Reef, Canyon lands, and

Arches which are located

In the Southern part of the state.

You can go river rafting, golfing,

See art festivals, culinary tourism,

Photo opportunities,

Discover quaint little towns,

Take scenic little side trips,

Or just find a place to relax.

By: Sharon Wiegand

Alaska

They have the coolest glaciers

And I hear they have a lot of bears

You can fish, watch animals or just

Look at the scenery.

There are lodges and cabins

You can stay at

I would image it would be better

To stay with a group

Than go on alone, you might get lost.

You can learn to cook

There are trips around the bay

See the tallest mountain

And you can spend the night in a tent.

By: Sharon Wiegand

Feeling the Comfort

When I wrap the lace around my shoulders

I feel the comfort of softness

It feels so extraordinary and special

It's very sexy next to my skin.

The warmth that I feel

Is so inviting and amazing to the depth

Of my soul

It takes my breath away.

I cannot project the feelings

Of details and techniques that

Intertwines the inter most highlights

That gives the feelings of comfort.

By: Sharon Wiegand

Timeless Traditions

Searching where all the timeless

Traditions have all began

Were made by mothers

Who were dedicated to satisfaction?

They started making things of lace

Beautiful shawls, scarves, tapestries,

Each one more appealing

Than the next

I wonder where these works

Of art began

But all I know,

It is a wonderful talent.

They are knitted by

Fantastic artists.

By: Sharon Wiegand

A Mother

I wish I had a mother to love

She lived to be very old

But I could never really talk to her.

She only wanted Dad.

He was her life.

He was everything to her.

He treated her badly.

And he was mean to her.

By: Sharon Wiegand

Many Christians

Many people pretend to be Christians

But they really are not;

They are truly flawed

With so many hidden sins.

I have so little faith

To be among them at all.

They criticize others

When they are so unscrupulous

Themselves.

Jesus is the one I look at

He is the one I praise

He is the one I emulate

He is the one I love.

By: Sharon Wiegand

Praise You

Without you, my Lord

I am weary

Without you, my Lord

I am sad

Without you, my Lord

I am sick

Without you, my Lord

I will die

I praise you, my Lord

You are mine

Forever,

Amen.

By: Sharon Wiegand

Give me the Strength

Give me the Strength to live

In this world of sin,

So bad, so sad,

I don't want to live

In a world so cruel

Take me to your heavenly world

Where love and happiness abide

Where Jesus loves me

And God loves me

Away from this Satan filled world.

By: Sharon Wiegand

Beyond the Pearly Gates

Will I see you?

Beyond the pearly gates

Amongst the crowd

Will I see you?

With extended arms

Will I see you?

Next to Jesus Christ

By: Sharon Wiegand

I Open My Arms

I open up my arms to you, my Lord

I give you all I have

I hope you know that all my dreams

Are centered on you each day

I don't waste my time on little things

Just on thoughts of you

I reach out to those who need a smile

And embrace those with sorrow in their eyes.

I've given all that I have and I don't

Have much more to give

The faith I have I pray each day

Is all I have to give?

By: Sharon Wiegand

Beyond Words

Give something priceless, your time

Share your professional skills

Give to your local mental health facilities

Support your local military families.

Give something valuable

To someone who is homeless

Give your first dollar

To the church on the corner.

Value each and every one you say hi too

And smile to every face that is crying

Give away your last dollar

And know that God will

Double its value.

Kiss the hand that you gave it too

Knowing God

Will bring you luck.

By: Sharon Wiegand

Jesus

Jesus will erase

The years of our life

He will bring us back

To a younger self.

We belong to God

We were born

Unto him as a child

And he will make

Us into a younger

Painless, self.

By: Sharon Wiegand

God

God will take away

Our pain and suffering

When I thought I had died

I felt no pain.

I wanted to live, then

Because I knew I

Was going to hell.

Because I had taken

My own life.

My Lord, My Lord

Listened to me

And gave me

Another chance

To redeem myself

And to change

My life.

Thank you

My Lord.

By: Sharon Wiegand

I Love my God

I Love my God

He gives me everything

I love him so

And I'm here for him.

Please wait for me

I want to be there God

Wait for me

I'm on my way.

I'm coming close to you

Guide me as I come near you

I am, near you, near you

All the way.

By: Sharon Wiegand

Erase Years

Get your body

Back into shape

Find a no-guesswork

Eating plan.

Walk around the corner

And the dream is yours

Find an exercise plan

And drink plenty of water.

Clear you mind

And just be patient.

By: Sharon Wiegand

Sweet Paradise

I'm waiting for you

Paradise

I'm longing for you

Paradise

I'm dreaming of you

Paradise

By: Sharon Wiegand

Spring

Daffodils display eyes among drifts

Looking among grassy hills and meadows

The curve impacts the side of mountains

Spreading around the farm land.

Doubling in size they command attention

They spread and illuminate the hillside

The meadows command attention

Impacting each moment it grows.

Blooming along the path of the highway

Displays its old fashioned bulbs

Knowing they will bloom next year

If you will otherwise keep them planted.

By: Sharon Wiegand

No Regrets

I have no regrets

I was blind sighted

I made a mess of things

I did the dumbest moves.

I look to God for forgiveness

I hope he will grant me a smile

And look from the heavens

And give me his word.

You are forgiven

You are my light

Walk in my path

And go forth my child.

By: Sharon Wiegand

Revitalize

Take time out

Take a laugh break

Read a good book

Reinvent yourself

Eat, pray, have peace of mind

Keep your family happy

Be a better person

Repair your skin

Redo your hair

Smooth you tootsies

Cream your hands

Nutrition your body

Supplement your mind

Lose the pounds

Support your heart

Organize your house

Love yourself

By: Sharon Wiegand

Chanel (Used to be #5)

I always wanted to buy

A bottle of Chanel perfume

But it was always to expensive

For me to invest in.

I would go by the counter

And wish my tastes

Weren't so expensive

To feel-good in.

I dreamed so many times

About that little bottle

Then realized my encounters

Were too far above my expectations.

By: Sharon Wiegand

Among the Magazines

I search the magazines

For perfect dress styles

But how many regular people

Wear them on the street.

I never see them on regular people

I only see them at church

Of course, I don't go anywhere

Except church.

I don't work

Because I'm a senior citizen

But I'd like to keep up on things

I'm a Facebook junky

And that's about it.

By: Sharon Wiegand

Obama's Challenge

The president has a historic challenge

To take a bold action on global warming

90 percent majority of Americans

Favor action on global warming.

The rise of the oceans are beginning

To slow and our planet has begun to heal

So please take us seriously

The loudest voice was hurricane Sandy.

It came and destroyed our coastline

Give us back our America

Help us to clean up our environment

It is a virtual emergency.

By: Sharon Wiegand

Obama's Climate Control

Our leader needs to clean up America

From the carbons in the air

To the solar energy on the buildings

Cutting the pollutions by 17 percent.

The scientists, engineers, and officials

Say we will have more hurricanes,

More tornadoes and more climate changes

Making our lives and environment more difficult.

Only God has what's left for us

Because he has predicted all of the above

In the last days before he comes

So I would just be prepared for him.

By: Sharon Wiegand

Lover

Speak only words of love

Speak only words of happiness

Don't let the words of hate

Breathe inside your door.

Love your partner as he

Loves you. Do not breathe

Words of hatred in your

Marriage. Remember that

Your dream of fairness lives

Inside your home. Try to

Stay focused. Try to remember

The words you said

On your wedding day.

Love, Honor, Respect.

By: Sharon Wiegand

Love

Love is an emotion,

A burning emotion,

A special feeling,

Holding your lover tight,

Kissing your lover on the lips,

Putting your arms around their waist,

Holding their hand,

Rubbing your lips on their body,

Doing something for them,

Telling the truth,

Wiping away their tears,

Smiling at them,

Opening the door,

Reading them a poem,

Sitting close to them,

Singing to them,

Cooking for them,

Praying with them,

Talking softly to them,

And being fair to them

By: Sharon Wiegand

My True Friend

I am your friend

Always close to you

I am there when you dream

Surrealistic so it seems

I would never make you cry

Or ever have the wisdom to try

And when the birds begin to sing

There would always be and angel with wings

And when the spirit was renewed with love

God would be there to sing from above

And when you had pain and sorrow

There would always be a cause to follow.

By: Sharon Wiegand

Secrets

Somber, secrets

Tender in your mind

Enlighten your supreme expressions

Remember with simply a smile.

Greet the human race

With beauty and faith

Sacrifice all your wishes

With tranquil reflections and tears.

Clutch that handkerchief close

When you are ready to say good night

There is a spiritual inspiration

That God's gathering peacefully tonight.

By: Sharon Wiegand

Neighbor Lady

My neighbor lady was a friend

As soft as a petal

As quiet as a newborn babe

As gentle as a soul

She was very kind

She always knew what was on my mind

Together we would dine

And her heart was all mine.

Sometimes I would look at her in disbelief

Because she always welcomed me with relief

When other kids would shout

She would say I like you without a doubt.

She would say she didn't like most kids

But she liked me no matter what I did

She said, "You are not like most kids"

"You are grown up and you're special."

By: Sharon Wiegand

Happiness

I have found happiness

In my own heart today

I am no longer obligated

On words others might say

I am my own per son

And I have the right

To depend solely on myself

When everything seems bright

I don't need to be pacified

Or to be tolerated by others

I do need to solely stand

On what, I believe

As I stand strongly alone

I wonder why I've asked

For so much acceptance

By all those I've known

By: Sharon Wiegand

Some Fish

As I sit on the riverbank,

I stretch out the fishing line

To catch myself some fish

Sitting in deep though,

I meditate and think

Of all the things I've lost

A pull on the line

Brings me back from afar

Guiding me to my fish

I reel in my catch

And throw out the line

To see what is biting

Hours go by

And I'm still waiting

For the biggest catch of all

By: Sharon Wiegand

The Rose

The petals of the rose

Slowly start to unfold

Gently as the sun touches

The petals and enlightens each one.

One by one they glide open

Turning the centers towards

The sun shining saying

"Hi" big world I'm smiling

"Look at me."

By: Sharon Wiegand

Wind

The wind stirred through the trees

Whisking up the dust beneath

The feet of the horses shuffling

The leaves around the bend.

Autumn had set in and the

Clear blue skies were turning gray

And the children were beginning

To rake up the leaves from the trees.

The leaves were turning different

Colors and falling from the trees

And the birds were chirping one

To another saying "let's go" and on they went.

By: Sharon Wiegand

Our Land

Gracious are the skies

That looks down upon the earth

They guard our ample land

And take care of the Heaven's above.

The land is ours forever

As long as we take care of what we have

It gives us shelter and a place to live

And an unending place to be.

As long as we take care of our planet

And appreciate where we live

The Heaven's and God above

Will keep a respectful earth below.

By: Sharon Wiegand

Smiling

A smiling face brings happiness

To me, in all its splendor

It gives pure delight in essence

And brings pleasure making life beautiful.

It speaks in words without speaking

Blossoming like a new spring flower

As if falling like rain from the sky

And piercing a broken heart.

A smiling face brings beauty out

Of the breeze of the wind

And caresses the body

Of a newborn baby when he looks upon our faces.

By: Sharon Wiegand

The Farmer

The farmer tills his soil

Caressing each seed

He places in the ground

Planting as he sows.

Riding on his tractor

He plows the ground

Underneath the soil

Growing plentiful

Unconditionally the sun

Attaches to the ground.

By: Sharon Wiegand

Help Us

You spilled the waters along the seacoast

We lost many homes and businesses

Bring back our dreams

We had for a brief moment.

You have taken our passion away

Give us back our livelihoods

We are broken and stuck in time

Give us our lives back to us.

God, we are struggling

Help us to get back to where we were

We need to return to yesterday

We have a lifetime to repair.

By: Sharon Wiegand

Leaves

The leaves have turned yellow

In the fall of October

And when they hit the ground

They turn brown.

They collected around the base

Of the tree and piled high

As the breeze began to collect

Around the blinding force of evil.

Lightning flashes flared in the sky

Striking the tree

Splitting the tree apart

Threatening its tall distance.

Down came the tall tree

Cutting it in half

Breaking the beauty

And existence-a thousand of years

By: Sharon Wiegand

My Brother

I wished I would have been there

To see you during your years

I know you were a great man

And you treated a lot of patients.

I wish I could have been there

To see you using your powerful

Hands to heal the sick and

To help them guide them in wonderful ways.

One day I'll see him in Heaven

And I'll get to talk to him

And I'll be there by his side

Again and we can talk.

By: Sharon Wiegand

God, Where Are You?

I look to the heavens for you

I look to the stars for you

I look to the church for you

I look to the sky for you

I look to the pastor for you

I look to the clouds for you

I look to the ground for you

I look everywhere for you

God I know you are in me.

By: Sharon Wiegand

Lonely Girl

The lonely girl sits alone

Waiting for someone to come along

She bats her eyes and looks around

For someone to look her way.

She has big brown eyes

Those swiftly move around

A glimmer of light shimmer from

Place to place and face to face.

She is a pretty little girl

She is sad and lonely

She is only 17 years old

Some day she will be a grown up girl.

By: Sharon Wiegand

Reflections

I know in myself I've loved God

I hope he loves me

I've tried to be a good person

And cherish my soul to God.

May God love me as I love him?

I will whisper Jesus words

And give them to God

And acknowledge everything he says.

Give me peace and I will follow

You all the days of my life

And I will follow Jesus words

As the bible says.

By: Sharon Wiegand

The Clock

The clock winds down every day

Darkness comes around this time

My husband kisses me and makes my dinner

I cry with tenderness at his thoughtfulness.

Before I choose to be worthy of his kindness

Such blessing I receive when my husband

Remembers me, and cook for me and takes

Care of me, and does wonderful things for me.

My mind is like a whirlwind ticking

Away, etching in time these memories

My husband has cherished for me

Whirling like a clock, ticking away.

By: Sharon Wiegand

I am Grateful

I am grateful for a home, a car,

Somewhere to sleep, somewhere to eat,

Somewhere to worship, a doctor to tell my problems to,

And a President to handle our problems.

I am grateful for God and Jesus to pray to and to take care

Of our problems,

I am grateful to stand strong for eternity,

And for never forsaking God's law,

I am here for my special love to

My husband and he will always be mine.

By: Sharon Wiegand

Arches

Underneath the broken arches

Lies the hearths that are broken

From the needles being pierced

Into the arms of broken bodies.

Bring back my sunken treasure

Of tears I've found in fragrance

In the brief times of moments

And the drops of moments gone by.

I've squirmed by such time I've felt

The needle, piece into my arm

Ouch it hurts, take it from my arm

But I guess there is a need for it this time.

By: Sharon Wiegand

Listen to the Words

I listen to the words in Matthew

They explain the birth and the death of Jesus

They tell about him rising from the dead

And being crucified on the cross.

I hope you've read the words

They tell about our Jesus

And what happened on the cross

And why Jesus is the Son to our God, Almighty One.

By: Sharon Wiegand

No Friends

I look around and I have no friends

No creatures dainty and graceful

No one to walk in the path of mine

And no one but to dine alone.

No one to fill my day with

No one to contemplate my life with

No one to remind of what a Creative genius I am

No one to give a flower to.

It would be nice to have a single friend

To say "Hi my pal, I'm glad to see you."

But instead I'm writing this sad poem

Wanting a friend like you.

By: Sharon Wiegand

Mother

You were there when I needed you

You were there when I grew up

But when I needed you most of all

You had died

And I had to walk alone.

By: Sharon Wiegand

Pictures

Frame up the memories in pictures

Takes the likeness and the essence

Stillness in a picture

Bring the innocence out in a picture.

Touch up the existence of the brightness

By preparing the lightness of the picture

Show the laughing qualities and the joyousness

And the infinite love desired in each picture.

By showing the deepest thoughts and those

Indifferences compared to the loneliness

Inside it is fun to learn about the reality

Of those whose feelings we have met.

By: Sharon Wiegand

Flowers

Bloom in the spring

And are so beautiful

You can pick one by one

Color by color, bright as the sun

They wilt with gloom

Stand in the rain and

In the sunshine

For they are truly grand

Red, blue, purple, gold

They stand at attention

Looking towards the sun.

By: Sharon Wiegand

5 Years Old

I'm 5 today

I'm growing big

I have a new brother

He is almost three

He is a big boy too

I'm a big girl too

I can take care of him

He is a good boy too

When I was only four

He was only two

We are good kids

Thank you God

For Everything!

By: Sharon Wiegand

Diana

Our angel married Prince Charles

On Wednesday 29th July 1981 at 11:00 a.m.

She was the Lady Diana Spencer

At the St. James's Palace, London.

Once upon a time Diana met her fella

And married him and dreary old

England were merry once more

Until Diana met her death.

Then merry old England were

Not happy anymore.

Millions of viewers watched her

Funeral and wished it never happened.

By: Sharon Wiegand

Diana, We See

Come back to your sons

They miss you so much

Your grand baby will be here soon

And we want you to be here.

Our hearts are with you in heaven

We grow each day with you

And your grandchildren will

Always know a piece of you.

Thank you for giving us

Your wonderful boys

They are very special and they are grand

We will always find you in them.

By: Sharon Wiegand

Come Back

We love you so, Diana

Come back to us, Diana

We see your smile, Diana

In your boys, Diana.

I know we will see you, Diana

The smiles in your grandchildren, Diana

The hopes and dreams, Diana

The eyes and understanding, Diana.

We miss you, Diana

But you will always be with us, Diana

Because we have your sons, Diana

And your grandchildren, Diana.

By: Sharon Wiegand

Sept.11, 2001

World Trade Center

New York City

Colleagues Scrambling

To meet deadlines

Two hijacked airlines

Ripped through the towers

Then the real horror

Was only beginning

Planes slam towers

Buildings collapsed

First world trade center downed

Then second one went down

Who was inside?

Will we ever know?

Why did they collapse?

By: Sharon Wiegand

Salvador Dali

Dali has the uncanny ability to

Get famous people to

Let down their guard

And to capture the essence

Of his subjects

Appearance and humility.

Dali likes to appear outside

The reality

Dali Atomicus is among the most

Famous portraits ever taken

From his

30 year collection.

By: Sharon Wiegand

Boom Boom

On December 21, 1988

Pan Am Flight 103

Exploded over Lockerbie, Scotland

Killing all 259 aboard

And 11 people on the ground.

The cause: homemade

Bomb consisting of a

Battery, an electronic

Timing device and

Less than a pound

Of plastique – a powerful,

Putty-like explosive

Invented by the British

During World War II.

By: Sharon Wiegand

Jackie Bouvier

A first Lady married

To John F. Kennedy

She was America's pillar of strength

And paragon of style.

She was an athlete from youth

She married Onassis in 1968

She cared mostly about being a mother

And worked as a book editor.

She battled to save landmarks

She had a stillborn daughter

She had a son who lived only three days

And she died at 64.

By: Sharon Wiegand

Amelia Earhart

A jaunty adventurer

Accomplished woman

Vanished above the South Pole

In twin-engine Lockheed

Electra, the type of craft

In which she perished.

Earhart was less confident

About matters of the heart

And found herself leaning

On a man, publisher

George Putman.

By: Sharon Wiegand

Eleanor Roosevelt

She was a world champion

Of human rights

She married her fifth cousin

Franklin Delano Roosevelt

In 1905 and bore 6 children

One of whom died in infancy.

In 1918 her husband was having

An affair with her social

Secretary Lucy Mercer.

Through months of soul-

Searching, she became a

Great and gallant-

Good lady – a powerful

Lady after her husband

Died.

By: Sharon Wiegand

Bonnie Parker

Shooting and looting

Clyde's sweetheart did it for love

She had a very short life

She saw herself as sensitive.

She was a poet

She had a talent for acting

She was smitten with Clyde

Clyde Barrow was all she craved.

She was 23 when she died

In Gilland, Louisiana

That was in 1934

That was after they made

The Ballad of Bonnie and Clyde.

By: Sharon Wiegand

Imelda Marcos

An ex-beauty queen

Her shopping sprees

Were the State's budget

She was not happy without

One pair of shoes

She was a poor girl.

She faced fraud

And racketeering charges

And was booted

Out of her country.

By: Sharon Wiegand

Song

Soothing, chirping melodies

Sing with clarity the birdies

Capturing the sounds wandering

In the sunset.

Voices in the night marking

The paths of tomorrow

And the promises stolen over

The ocean in the dark.

Ceaseless time drift away in

The night from memory of Robin's

And warbled in the clear

Voices bring crystal clear tonight.

By: Sharon Wiegand

Love to You

How far away are the nights?

I miss you.

The days are filling with sorrow

As the tide has ruled the sea.

I miss you far into the boundaries

Of days that are filled with ecstasy

I feel the truth of catch the tides

Of the passions that fill our love.

The earth, the openness, the truth,

The mind over matter, the cracks in the sidewalks

Even though we are living on the edge

I love you even then.

By: Sharon Wiegand

Pets

Our dreams came true when our first

Little one came into our life

And then the second one came out

And both of them were dogs.

The first was a Burmese Mountain Dog

And the second was a Cocker Spaniel Dog.

We love them both each and every day

And they became more than our pets.

We call them our children now

And we love them very much.

We hope to never lose our children

Because we can never part with them.

By: Sharon Wiegand

Bonnie

What a big dog she is?

Brown, black, and white she is.

She is a beautiful girl

And we are proud of her.

She watches TV everyday

And barks at the animals

On TV and also looks out the

Window and barks at suspects, one might see.

She plays with her brother Champ

Who is three, but Champ is the boss

Even though

He is a year younger than she.

By: Sharon Wiegand

Snowmaker

The snow is falling

And dissolving outside

Romantically and insignificant

And accepts the white stillness.

Slowly the snow

Begins to slow down

And the sparkling white sight

Was very bright like Christmas Day.

In winter, I see the beauty

In granny's white hair

And find beauty in everything

Such as her sweet gingerbread cookies.

By: Sharon Wiegand

My Swing

My swing hangs below my tree

The tree is so big

I try to climb it

And it is so big

I can't get down.

I call my mother

To help get me down

Because I can't get down

By myself.

By: Sharon Wiegand

Sweet Angel

When I came to you in the darkness

I prayed that you would let me live

I knew I wasn't going to heaven

But to hell.

The darkness frightened me

Because I knew my soul within

I knew my journey was very long

And there was no peace for me at all.

I've tried to make up but you know

The music will not be playing my song

Because my conscience still bothers me,

I don't feel that sweet angel near.

By: Sharon Wiegand

Love You

I love you when I am sleeping

I love you when I am awake

I love you every time of the day

I love you in between those other times.

You have taken care of me

When I was sick

You have taken care of me

When I was home.

You were there to issue my pills

You were there to cook my food

You were there to put me to bed

You were there to kiss my cheek.

You are my one and only

I love you so much

Thank you for everything

You mean so much to me.

By: Sharon Wiegand

Animals

The tigers are running

Across the land

Running away from

Human hands.

Wanting to survive

From the wild

Humans with

Bows and arrows.

Save me their

Hearts are saying

Inside or we'll

Be extinct one day.

By: Sharon Wiegand

Teacher

A teacher is like gold

She never leaves your mind

She silently is like a rainbow

At the end of every street.

She is like song of freedom

And the rose within its beauty

She was always bright and cheerful

Almost blinding; she was so bright.

By: Sharon Wiegand

Window

Sitting by the window
Of our Sun Lakes club
Showcased our pictured
Window at night.

What a beautiful
Night it was
Looking through that
Window at the patio.

We have for guests
When we have bingo
During breaks
To smoke and to talk.

The lights were
Breaking through the
Fireplace and lamps to show
The exquisite furniture
Along with the paintings.

By: Sharon Wiegand

Stars

Illuminating from above

They sparkle endlessly in the sky

They brighten up the night

And bring softness into our eyes.

The memories are so sweet

They heighten our lifetime

Of joyfulness and happiness

Saying we cherish you.

We love the brightness it

Brings into our hearts

And will always look to

Our stars that guide us in the night.

By: Sharon Wiegand

Bermuda Triangle

Supposedly they say

Ships have disappeared

In the deep waters surrounding

The Bermuda Triangle.

The apexes are drawn between

San Juan, Puerto Rico, Miami,

And of course Bermuda

They say the waters are haunted.

Are they cursed or is it just

Rife with ill fate

We will never know – what

Brought them to their mysterious end.

By: Sharon Wiegand

Blue Whale

It is the largest animal

To inhabit the earth

It can grow to 105 feet in length

And 200 tons in weight.

The whale's tongue is large

Enough for 5 people to stand on it.

It drinks 50 gallons of its mother's milk each day

Gaining about 200 pounds a day.

By: Sharon Wiegand

Hummingbird

They have a high breathing rate

And body temperature is the highest

Rate of metabolism of any

Animal on the planet.

They consume one half

Or more of its body weight

In nectar each day.

That means regular feedings are mandatory.

They visit flowers or feeders

Between five and eight times an hour

The smallest is the bee hummingbird;

The largest is the albatross hummingbird.

By: Sharon Wiegand

Loch Ness Monster

Has shown up many places

Some believe it's true

Some people believe it's false

It's never been proven.

It has been reported in lakes and oceans

And there have been many sightings

But the scientists have declared

That there is no such monster.

Believe in what you may

It's up to the believer

What did you see?

In the waters you questioned.

By: Sharon Wiegand

Clinton

Played his saxophone

Battled republicans in Congress

He met President Kennedy

And was inspired to enter politics.

He was elected governor in Arkansas

At 32 serving 3 terms

And becoming a dynamic leader

And then became president.

Despite allegations of adultery

And avoiding the draft

During the Vietnam War

He was a successful president.

By: Sharon Wiegand

An Angel's Voice

I heard an angel's voice

It must be my sister who died.

She tells me she misses me

And wonders where I am.

I didn't see her

Before she died;

In fact, I hadn't seen

Her since I was a child.

And now I hear her

Whisper in my ear;

I haven't forgotten you

My dear, you are still in my heart.

By: Sharon Wiegand

George W. Bush

Bush was elected president

After capturing the nomination

As he promised to run a morally

Upright campaign.

He told the citizens he offered

"Prosperity with a purpose."

He promised to cooperate

With the Democrats.

He said he was capable

Of pleasing people without

Regard to their race, gender,

Or class.

By: Sharon Wiegand

My Heart

My heart belongs to you

Every minute of the day

Every hour of the day

Every day of the month.

My heart belongs to you

During the day you are a treasure

During the night you are a gem

All the time you are everything.

You are overwhelming

And when you twinkle an eye

My love grows stronger

Each and every day.

By: Sharon Wiegand

George Bush

He was the first incumbent

Vice president elected

Since Martin Van Buren.

The first president to have been

Director of the Central Intelligence Agency.

He was a World War II veteran

Youngest pilot in the US Navy to

Flying 58 combat missions against

The Japanese and won

Distinguished Flying Cross for Bravery.

By: Sharon Wiegand

Alzheimer's

My mother fought the cruel clutch

Of that heartless disease;

That cares so little about one's life

Slowly, it takes your life away from you.

Not knowing who your family or friends are

All you have is just a stare

An empty stare with nothing in your mind

Just confusion, emptiness, and sad feelings.

Who are you?

Once your mind was clear, sharp, and bright

Now it's unoccupied

It contains nothing, it's gone forever.

By: Sharon Wiegand

Cursed Mary Celeste

103 feet 282 ton launched in 1861

Off Nova Scotia within days her captain died.

During this maiden voyage she collided

With another ship and her hull was damaged.

The owner who tried to salvage her went bankrupt.

She was repaired and returned to service in 1872.

On Nov. 5 the Mary Celeste set out from NYC

For Genoa, Italy with a cargo of commercial alcohol.

Days later she was drifting like a drunken sailor.

The Mary Celeste was boarded and founded to be

Deserted save for her cargo and a store of food.

Where had all the people gone?

We likely will never know.

By: Sharon Wiegand

Sliding Glass Window

As I was reading a passage

In the bible

A ray of light shined through

Our sliding glass window.

I knew God was speaking to me say

"I'm here, listen to me."

I felt an unusual feeling in the pit of my stomach

Because I knew God was there with me.

By: Sharon Wiegand

Footprints in the Snow

As I walk through the snow

I find snowflakes falling

On the ground like memories

Making footprints in the snow.

Many years ago, my children

Made angel wings in the snow

And I recall as I am walking

Making footprints in the snow.

And if snowflakes were transparent

And landed complacent in time

I would remember my children

Making footprints in the snow.

By: Sharon Wiegand

Mark

Mark, my son

He is the best

Guy around

He once was a little boy

Now he is a grown up man.

I'm so proud of him

And that I'm his mom.

He is a husband now

And I can't boss him around

I am so lucky

I have a daughter-in-law.

By: Sharon Wiegand

Champ

His eyes are big and round

And brown.

He is always running

Around the ground.

He is my favorite dog.

He is almost like a toy.

He sleeps with me on the bed

And keeps my feet warm at night.

By: Sharon Wiegand

Freedom

Is a big price we all pay?

The soldiers give their lives

Every day to pay for us

To live in a free society.

While we take advantage

Of what we have at home

Our boys are giving their lives

For what we take for granted.

Freedoms are we really free?

By: Sharon Wiegand

Audrey Hepburn

The lithe beauty of stylish romance

Became UNICEF special ambassador

To world's underprivileged children

And she died in 1993.

She was naturally emotionally charming

And she cared about the world

And she wished she had curves like other females

But she was very compassionate.

By: Sharon Wiegand

Shirley Temple

Shirley Temple was a very bright young child

She became an angel to an ambassador

She married a navy man Charlie Black

And she became an Ambassador.

She became very popular in politics

And was a first class mother

She had a career in diplomacy

And became interested in the real world.

By: Sharon Wiegand

Julia Roberts

She was a Georgia peach

And she was a pretty woman

Everybody loved her

And has that beautiful smile everyone loves.

She was married a couple of time

But now she has a couple of kids

Everybody loves her

Because she is our pretty woman.

By: Sharon Wiegand

Mary Tyler Moore

She is Danny Thomas 's Daughter

And she raises money for the kids with cancer

She helps them out

Cause they get sick.

She was on TV in the 1970

On the Mary Tyler Moore Show

And it was very popular

And her father was on it.

She is a female comedian

And is very funny

We all love her

When we see her.

By: Sharon Wiegand

Tammy Wynette

Was a country singer

I liked her very much

She sang heartbreaking songs

About her breakups.

Most of them were about George Jones

Because they broke up so many times

But they always got back together

And were happy sometimes.

Her stories were happy and sad

But she always sang very nicely

Her first marriage ended

But she moved on to Nashville.

By: Sharon Wiegand

Gracie Allen

George Burns and Gracie Allen spent time together

And had a lot of fun together

And when they fooled around together

They sang a lot of memorable songs.

Their careers bloomed when

They were together

Marry me or I'll break up the act.

That's what kept them together

Many years.

By: Sharon Wiegand

Sophia Loren

So pretty was she.

She kept the boys.

Going until it was three.

And when there was a beauty contest

She was always there

Because she was always so pretty

And glamorous

To all the boys

She was the favorite one.

By: Sharon Wiegand

Phoenix

How beautiful I do see

The furniture in the showrooms in your collections.

I inspire to measure the styles that exist among your shapes

They design exactly what I desire.

Generous are the convenient on-site examples

Finest are the features and finishes

Selected by the region's best regard designers

By: Sharon Wiegand

Sally Ride

Our first woman astronaut

Who was chosen for Challenger

And was killed over Texas as it was

Being launched.

Many laughs were being

Stressed because a woman

Was on the Challenger

Saying they were holding up the

Launch because a woman was looking

For a purse to match her space shoes.

By: Sharon Wiegand

A Gentle Kiss

I get much energy
From your sweet kiss
I get a great feeling of warmth
And a compelling sensation

The eagerness of your lips
Brings such romance to me
As you bring out fiery emotions
My passion becomes so alive

I feel so much appreciation
From those lips that are delicate
And softly expressing your love
I'm deeply among your sentiments

The burning zeal that comes to me
From your total irresistible attention
Gives me an enamored sense of love
And respect of such strength

By: Sharon Wiegand

Price is Right

We went to the Price is Right

And my husband fell on the ground

I didn't know if he was hurt

And then they put us at the front of the line.

Then when we got up there

They told us we could not be picked because

We weren't sister and brother

And that made my husband really mad.

It never said on the tickets we had to be

Brother and sister or we

Would never have come to the show.

My husband was really mad.

Because we drove a long way

To get there.

And they said we could stay but we could

Not go on stage.

I had brought him my books I had written

Plus a plate I had painted plus a

Thing I had painted for his wife.

And I just gave it to the guy and just said.

Give this to Drew.

I made this especially for him.

And we went home.

And I felt real bad.

By: Sharon Wiegand

Marie Curie

Born in Warsaw in 1867

The youngest of five children

She toiled as a governess for a Polish family

She married a physics professor whom she met in Paris

In 1895 He was killed by a horse drawn carriage in 1906

She had 2 young daughters and became a professor

She died in 1934 from exposure from radiation

She once wrote "There is nothing in my acts,"

"Which obliges me to feel diminished?"

By: Sharon Wiegand

Marilyn Monroe

The blonde bombshell

She had the heart of a little girl

With a platinum wig

And she wanted to be protected.

She longed desperately to have children

Her sister said she had one leg longer than the other

She had a mole that she colored with an eye pencil

And her mother had spent many years in a mental hospital.

Joe DiMaggio loved her

And was very good to her

She was 28 when she was married to him

But could not escape her pill addiction.

By:

Sharon Wiegand

Beautiful Eyes

Beautiful are the eyes that I see

They are luminous and brilliant

I love to look in your eyes so bright

And so lucent and highlighted.

How I long to kiss the corners of the edges

Of the eyes that are beaming so brightly

And are attached to the brilliancy

Of the brim of the eyes.

I love the eyes that give the buoyant

Color of the eye

And bring such luster

And give me so much promise.

By: Sharon Wiegand

130

Senses

The senses of your smell is a fragrance

Of an unknown odor just only of you

No other person has that smell only you

It's a fragrance that only is in you.

I smell it every time I get close to you.

It is just a strong and unusual smell.

I can't get it out of my mind.

It's so wonderful and gentle and personal.

My wonderful honey, you are mine.

Your senses are in my mind.

They corrupt my mind.

They endure my mind.

You are my endless impressible one.

You take my heart away.

You are my articulate one.

And I love you so much.

By: Sharon Wiegand

Incandescence

Have you seen a hot body?

Most guys are looking for a gleaming body.

If they go into a bar they see a hot girl.

But if they stay home they can see one too.

Make sure you fix up nice

Then they won't go out

And your man will stay at home

Where he belongs.

By: Sharon Wiegand

Letter

I'm beginning to forget what a letter

Was and how personal it was

Now every one reads your mail

Of course the mailman used to read it.

Sometimes the post office would read it

If you had a small post office

Or if it had to be inspected

Or if the government had to check it.

There are all kinds of reasons why

It may have to be read at the

Post office or by the mailman

So don't get upset if it's read.

By: Sharon Wiegand

Love him

Love him in all that you do

Be strong and courageous

Seek him in all you do

And he will show you the path.

He will not fail nor abandon you

He will personally go ahead of you

Trust in the Lord your God

He will bring happiness in your life.

By: Sharon Wiegand

Blue Eyes

The color of your eyes

Are so perfectly designed

They have the purest color

Of blue I've ever seen.

They show so much compassion

And sensitivity to those around

Gentleness encompasses them

When understanding is allowed.

I've grown so accustomed

Of feeling much admired

By the softness of the amorous

Big, blue eyes.

By: Sharon Wiegand

Memories

Memories are made of happiness

Of joy, pleasure, and satisfaction

Memories that last a lifetime

Are conveyed by a special feeling

Looking back on all the photographs

That we spent so many years securing

Knowing that someday in the future

Those pictures would be there to share

Reading all those old letters

That was written to each of us

Brings about so many old feelings

Knowing how beautiful life has been

How special are the memories

That the two of us have shared

We look to the future knowing

Our lives have been complete.

By: Sharon Wiegand

Snowflakes

My vacation is here at last,

We're going to a place far away

The mountains are lily-white

And falls among the trees.

The coldness stands our hair on ends

Waiting for winter to begin,

We're dressed in warm attire

Getting frostbite from the snow.

The wind is blaring down on us,

Cold chills attack my depleted body,

The cloudy skies above me

Are defiantly gloomy and overcast

Lacking brightness among the clouds,

Tiny snowflakes multiply on the ground

Bringing a pure white carpet

Full of softness and gentleness

By: Sharon Wiegand

The Artist and the Easel

The artist sits while she creates

An easel full of brilliant colors

The brush glides effortlessly along

The canvas designing a picture

The artist sits quietly examining

The work she has produced

She gives it the once over

And is content with the likeness

As she garnishes the picture

With delicate strokes,

Her noticeable representation

Is absolutely drawn to perfection

By: Sharon Wiegand

My Father

Take me home, my father,

To that beautiful place

Where flowers abound

And friends are all around

Each person is the same

No rank, color, or separation

Where we live in harmony

And suffer no shame.

No bodies to weight us down

No words to bring a frown

Only happiness we share

And nothing to bear

I am waiting for

This beautiful sound

That calls me

To you loving arms

By: Sharon Wiegand

I Remember You

As I look into a crowd

I see images of you

And when I dream

I always think of you.

Those delightful eyes

Pierce my dwelling soul

I look up in the sky

And I remember you

Never a day goes by

Without thought of you

My wonderful guy

I remember you

By: Sharon Wiegand

Father, Hear My Plea

My Lord, My God,

Teach me how to love,

Somewhere deep down inside

Has taken that ability away.

Guide me to be your disciple,

Spreading the truth of your words,

Help direct me on the right track,

And shield me from all sins.

I want to spend time with you

Every day of my life,

Dedicating my existence

To you in every way.

I need the power

To fight all the evils

That constantly plagues

My everyday existence.

Please take my hand

And feel the sincerity

That all my dreams

Exist only for you.

By: Sharon Wiegand

My Lord, My God,

Send me an angel

To monitor my actions

And keep me safe.

Help guide me

In making difficult decisions

And teach me, My Lord,

To be a Disciple for you

I look up to you

For guidance and strength

Please let me understand

What is required of me?

Thank you for giving us,

Jesus to comfort us

And to make us realize

Heaven is around the corner

By: Sharon Wiegand

Looking for You

Among the distant crowd

Beyond the glittering faces
With an anxious glance
I am looking for you

How I miss your glorious smile

Your hand upon mine

Feeling your warmth beside mine

I am looking for you

Sadly, I remember those days

When the two of us were together

Sharing quiet moments

I am looking for you.

Come back to me, my love

I will bring you flowers

And give you all my love

I am still looking for you.

By: Sharon Wiegand

Time Alone

Time alone can bring

Comfort to your soul,

It gives you space

To examine your life.

Time alone soothes

Your active mind,

It gives you the freedom

To examine your thoughts

Time alone relieves

The stress of the day

It brings, peace, contentment,

And solace to your emptiness

Time eases the load

When nothing else can provide,

The tranquility you deserve

To heal your inner self

By: Sharon Wiegand

Made in the USA
Charleston, SC
18 February 2013